First Steps in Following Christ

First Steps in Following Christ

A Workbook for Growing Christians

Lloyd O. Bowen

Foreword by Arlo F. Newell

warner press®

Anderson, Indiana

Warner Press, Inc.
PO Box 2499
Anderson, IN 46018-2499
800-741-7721
www.warnerpress.org

ISBN-13: 978-1-59317-577-1

Printed in the United States of America.

warner press®

Table of Contents

Foreword

Being spiritually "born again" (John 3:3) is a thrilling experience in the life of an individual and the church. Jesus used this term to signify a radical change in one's life in which "old things have passed away; behold, all things have become new" (2 Cor 5:17). This kind of experience creates joy in heaven, making the angels sing (Luke 15:7). Likewise, the local church should celebrate conversion even more than growth in attendance. We ought to ask ourselves, Has anyone been saved here recently? If so, have we sufficiently helped them to begin a life of healthy spiritual development?

You see, being "born again" is only the beginning of a changed life; we must help converts become established in their newfound faith and develop a mature faith for the future. Our high spiritual mortality rate constrains us to guide the first steps of new disciples as they seek to follow Jesus Christ. Lloyd Bowen's book addresses this need.

Following Christ is not an easy road, but this workbook provides thirteen practical studies to help a new Christian in critical areas of need. Lloyd Bowen has a passion for helping congregations conserve new converts and sustain those who struggle to survive in today's culture. These lessons have been tested and proven successful in developing healthy disciples.

If you are one of these new believers, the following questions may come to mind:

> *Who is this book for?* The First Steps workbook is for any person who wants to follow Christ faithfully. What may appear impossible at the beginning of your journey will become possible, one step at a time. This study helps you move forward at your own speed, enabling you to measure your spiritual growth along the way.
>
> *What help will this book give me?* Each step of the discipleship process is clearly outlined in scripture and personal example. Christ becomes your mentor, walking with you wherever you may be. Your sourcebook is the Bible itself, and the path of study is clearly marked for you. The secret? Keep your eyes on Christ, for he alone is your example and leader.
>
> *How can I do all of this?* First Steps shows you how to develop a daily discipline of obedience to God. You will memorize scripture and apply it to your daily life. In so doing, you will become strong in the Lord. And you will

be reminded that you are not alone on the journey. Christ is your guide, and he has never failed anyone who followed him.

Where will Christ lead me? He leads you to unity with other believers like yourself. You may find it in a Bible study group, a parachurch group, or a local congregation. In any of these contexts, Christian fellowship will help you build your faith. Walking in Christ's footsteps will lead to a victorious Christian life, for as you live in the Word, you will be able to live in the world. Your life will then become an example and influence to draw others to know Christ.

A final word to the pastor: I recommend that you give a copy of *First Steps* to each new convert under your ministry. Give it to others who have been "in the Way" for several years but still need to become mature in Christ. Encourage them to join a small group where they will grow in their personal relationship with the Lord.

Arlo F. Newell
Editor in Chief Emeritus
Warner Press, Inc.
Anderson, Indiana

Acknowledgments

The gestation period of this book has been a very long one. In many ways, this material is a personal and theological journey that spans more than four decades. Tucked into these pages are several personal references. For me personally, this has been a wonderful journey toward spiritual, relational, and theological wholeness and maturity. The material has been gathered from several sources, and each of them has flowed through my soul and mind for several years. Though I have borrowed from a few people whom I remember, a large quantity of the material has become so much incorporated in me that I have no idea of its original references.

There are a few important sources that I used in preparing these lessons. I want to acknowledge these.

First, I have adapted materials from Dr. David Grubbs's notebook *Evangelism That Works*, which he called "Basic Christian Living." I am deeply indebted to him for some of the lesson content, which has been modified for my use. I have much gratitude in my heart for his expressed, written permission to use substance from that which he developed.

In Step 5, I borrowed some ideas from William Parker and Elaine St. John's book *Prayer Can Change Your Life*. Some of their ideas provided inspiration, though I did not quote directly from their work. I am indebted to them for spurring me on in my discoveries and my growth in prayer.

In Step 7, the materials under the caption "How to Read Devotionally" were adapted from chapter 13 of Kenneth E. Jones's book *Let's Study the Bible*. I am thankful for the permission granted by his grandson.

The materials used in Step 10, III, "Guidelines for Christian Financial Freedom," were adapted from materials that were given to me by James C. Green. He has graciously given his permission for these materials to be used in this volume.

These are the sources which I quoted and from which I knowingly borrowed. But I am also grateful to others who have graciously shared ideas and reflections with me in working with our common purpose—to see believers get started right and come to productive maturity in Christ. If I have overlooked any source, I sincerely seek the indulgence of that person or entity.

I am keenly aware of this book's limitations. I wished to include more teaching materials in this work about the Holy Spirit's ministries in the individual believer and in the body of Christ. The ministries of the Holy Spirit are implied throughout, but I yearned for more direct teaching about Him and His work among us. There were places in the manuscript when I wanted to widen my focus, but space would not permit me to do so.

I have sought to synthesize these materials into what I believe is consistent with that which God is calling us together to do in making disciples. It is one thing to be a spiritual baby. It is quite another to be a balanced, productive, mature, reproducing disciple of Jesus Christ. It is my heart's desire to provide some fresh approaches for young believers (whatever their age) to claim the promises of God and to walk by faith as a lifestyle. I am aware that there is repetition at various points in this volume, but I felt this might be beneficial for young believers in their quest for maturity.

I am deeply indebted to Joseph Allison and Stephen Lewis for the patience and editorial gifts that they demonstrated in grooming this material for publication. In addition, I am grateful to Becky Fauntleroy for sharing her thoughts with me and making helpful suggestions regarding the manuscript. I am also immensely appreciative of my wife Vonda's partnership in life, in the gospel, and in the use of her creative and editorial gifts. Without her assistance, this project would not have been completed.

Lloyd O. Bowen
Anderson, Indiana

Introduction

The purpose of this course is to help you grow into the spiritual likeness of Jesus Christ. During these thirteen weeks, we will ask you to be completely honest with God and with yourself. This will mean doing things that may be unfamiliar or seem to take special effort on your part, but everything asked of you will be for this purpose.

Your mentor or group leader has set up a tentative schedule for the coming weeks. How closely you follow the agenda will depend on you and your needs. Remember that the ultimate goal is to help you learn the skills you need for an effective Christian life.

Even though there may be a great age span in your discipleship group, you have one thing in common—you are all Christ-followers. This one fact will enable you to work together meaningfully. Anticipate learning things you can pass along to other Christians, to continue this process of discipleship well into the future.

This workbook contains the lesson outlines for the entire course. Use it for taking notes, for refreshing your memory between class sessions, and for periodic review after you have completed the course. Look up the Bible references at home and take time to meditate on them, prayerfully asking, "Lord, how does this Bible passage apply to my life?" A free online study guide is availalble at http://alturl.com/ekn2u.

Although our first session seems tailor-made for new believers, it contains valuable insight for those who have been Christians for many years. It explains how a person becomes a Christ-follower, and it answers the question, How can I know that I belong to Christ? So don't skip the first session, no matter how long you have been a Christian. It lays an important foundation for understanding what will follow.

Step 1
Newborn in Christ

Key Verse

"Therefore, if anyone is in Christ, he is a new creation; old things have passed away; behold, all things have become new." —2 Corinthians 5:17

Introduction

We accept the fact that newborn babies need to develop, both physically and mentally. A baby cannot walk, talk, or do much of anything—except eat, cry, and depend on others. Babies cannot make their own plans for the future, defend themselves from harm, nor do many other things that mature persons do.

As time goes by, we expect to see signs of growth and development: First, a baby notices your hand moving in front of her eyes; she learns to coo; she rolls over for the first time; she grips your finger. We are eager to see the baby develop. We try to mold that child into a healthy person as best we can. We get excited about her development and tell anyone who will listen about her progress. We should anticipate a similar pattern of growth in our spiritual life.

In John 3:1–8, Christ spoke about new disciples as people who have been "born again." The apostles Peter and Paul referred to new Christians as "new creations" or "babes in Christ" (note our key verse and 1 Peter 2:2–3). In other words, at the beginning of our discipleship, we are nothing more than newborn Christ-followers. This is important to understand, because we may feel we are ready to take on the world, but we are not. We have a lot of growing to do.

Bible Study

I. What are the steps to being born again (becoming a new person in Christ)?

A. **Faith**—trusting wholly in what Christ has done for us on the cross.

1. The faith that saves us is not simply a "temporal faith" (i.e., head knowledge) that says, in effect, "Yes, I know that God created the universe, and I know that Jesus was a good man."

   According to James 2:19, who believe and fear?

   ____

   ____

   These beings have temporal faith (i.e., they know who Jesus is), but are they saved?

   ____

   ____

2. Even trusting in our "good works" is not enough. How do our best works look in the sight of the holy God? (See Isaiah 64:6.)

   ____

   ____

   If we are not saved by trying to do good, then what saves us? (See Titus 3:5.)

   ____

   ____

3. Notice how Jesus describes the "works" which His followers are to do (John 6:28–29). Describe these works in your own words:

   ____

   ____

4. Acts 16:30 describes how a Philippian jailer came to a couple of Christians, asking what he must do to be saved. Put Paul and Silas's answer in your own words (16:31).

____

____

5. The jailer's experience demonstrates that we must have faith in order to be saved. This faith is totally trusting in Christ and what He did for us by dying on the cross for our sins. Saving faith is further explained by Philippians 3:8-9. Summarize these two verses in your own words:

____

____

____

____

B. **Repentance**—turning your life around.

1. The New Testament Greek word that is translated as "repent" literally meant to "turn around," to "return," or "to have a change of heart and mind." To repent implies a definite change of your life's direction. If you are running from life, from your problems, from your inner self, from God's good plan for your life, then repentance occurs when you turn and face that from which you have been running—including God Himself.
2. Repentance involves remorse and sorrow. However, it is more than feeling sorry for "running away." It is letting your heart be broken for your sins, just as Christ's heart was broken for you and your sins when He died on the cross for you. In 2 Corinthians 7:8–11, the apostle Paul tells how he made the Corinthians sad (or grieved) so that they would change their attitudes and behaviors. What does he call the grief that will produce that change (7:9)?

____

____

What does he say that this kind of sorrow leads to? (7:10)

On the other hand, Paul says this kind of sorrow does not lead to regret or despair. Why do you suppose it doesn't?

3. When we turn from our sinful ways, what does God do with our sins? (Acts 3:19)

4. For a different perspective, what does Psalm 103:12 say that God does with our sins?

5. In 1 John 1:9, we have a promise. If we confess our sins/our wrongs/our failures to God, what two essential things will God do for us?

6. Can we be sure that God will do this? Why or why not?

C. **Obedience**—doing what God directs you to do.

1. Once your heart and mind have been changed (through repentance), you have a mind to obey the Lord. That readiness to follow through on what God has said is what gives a Christ-follower peace and purpose.

You know your sins are forgiven and you are a new person in Christ. Read Ephesians 2:8–10 and summarize its meaning.

____

____

____

____

2. A Jewish leader named Nicodemus asked Jesus what he must do in order to be saved (John 3:1–8). He was ready to obey God, but what did Jesus say needed to happen before he could obey?

____

____

II. How can we be sure that we belong to Christ?

We may not always feel that we are Christ-followers, but **our feelings cannot be trusted.** God's promises can be trusted. Here is what God's Word says about our new life in Christ and how we can be sure that we have been born again.

A. John 6:47 declares that the one who ______________ has (right now) eternal life.

B. John 1:12: Did you receive Christ as your Savior? ______ Then God promised you sufficient power or the right to become a ______________.

C. Romans 5:1 declares that since Christ has made us right in God's sight, we have a special gift. What is it? ____________

D. Romans 8:16 gives us further assurance. Who speaks to us in the core of our being that we are, in fact, children of God?

____

____

E. Romans 10:13 adds further encouragement. Did you call on the name of the Lord for forgiveness of your sins? _______ Then with this promise you know for sure that you are _________________________________.

F. More encouragement is found in 1 John 3:14. This passage declares that we know we have passed from death into eternal life because ____________________________.

G. Read Revelation 3:20. Explain in your own words how this word picture applies to your life.

____

____

Summary

Recall the time you came to Christ. What did you turn from and what did you turn to? You might say you felt better afterward, but why? Because the feeling of guilt was lifted when you confessed that you had done wrong? Is that what we mean when we say you have been "born again" or "saved"? This is part of the answer, but not all of it.

Repentance means turning from a life of sin dedicated to pleasing self to begin a life of pleasing God. Rebirth comes when we allow Christ to enter our lives by faith to lead and control us. We are forgiven for our past and armed by Christ's Holy Spirit for the future. We are made sons and daughters of God. When we are born again, we make a complete change in our life direction.

It is wonderful to know that your sins are forgiven and you are a child of God. You are beginning an eventful journey. Keep with it and grow in it.

Home Assignments

For further thought and encouragement, share your personal journey with someone this week. Other people need what you have discovered. That does not mean you will never stumble or fall, but you are learning to walk as a small child learns to walk.

- Read John 3:1–8 and 1 John 5:13–15, 18–20..
- Memorize the Key Verse (2 Corinthians 5:17).
- Look ahead at next week's material. It will make you excited about being in class next week.

Step 2

Dealing with Temptation

Key Verse

"No temptation has overtaken you except such as is common to man; but God is faithful, who will not allow you to be tempted beyond what you are able, but with the temptation will also make the way of escape, that you may be able to bear it." —1 Corinthians 10:13

Introduction

When we gave ourselves to Christ, we became overcomers. "For whatever is born of God overcomes the world. And this is the victory that has overcome the world—our faith. Who is he who overcomes the world, but he who believes that Jesus is the Son of God?" (1 John 5:4–5). However, this victory is won through conflict, and sometimes we will be sorely tested. We must "fight the good fight of faith" to win (1 Tim 6:12). It would be tragic to assume that we will not be tempted or that we would not fall back into sin.

But our God can equip us to face any adversary. Scripture says He will not let us be tried more than we can withstand with His help. In fact, He can turn our trials into opportunities for real spiritual growth and blessing if we continue to trust and obey Him.

However, if you falter in the struggle with temptation, you have an "Advocate with the Father, Jesus Christ, the Righteous" (1 John 2:1). He will forgive, cleanse, and strengthen you. God invites you to renew your commitment to Him and turn your back on sin. Continuing to do anything that you know displeases God will break your fellowship with Him. A Christ-follower simply cannot continue to practice sin (1 John 3:9).

Beginning a new life with Christ was wonderful; but overcoming temptation with Him day by day is even better. You see His faithfulness demonstrated continually and you learn that, no matter what comes your way, His grace is sufficient to sustain you. God never stops loving you. As the hymn writer William C. Poole said more than a century ago:

> Just when I need Him, Jesus is near;
> Just when I falter, just when I fear;
> Ready to help me, ready to cheer;
> Just when I need Him most.[1]

It was God's daily practice to meet Adam in the cool of the day and talk with him (Gen 3:8ff). The Bible records that Enoch walked with God. He disappeared because God took him away (Gen 5:24). Abraham had the reputation of being a friend of God (2 Chron 20:7). Just as God met these people in the middle of their daily life circumstances, so He meets us now. When we are in a great battle, He comes to us, and when the battle is over, He will come and minister to us again with spiritual refreshment. Yes, he met Mary at the tomb and Simon Peter at the seaside and the two men who were on their way to Emmaus on that first Resurrection Day. He continues to meet with us in all of life when He is invited to do so. We always need God's senior partnership.

Bible Study

I. Tempted by our spiritual Enemy

Though we will be severely tested, the Bible assures us that Jesus has promised us victory. Let's learn to trust in Him and in what He has said.

A. What does the Bible say about temptation? Look up the following Scripture references and then restate them in your own words.

1. 1 Peter 5:8

   a) Who is your chief spiritual Enemy?

   ____

   ____

1. "Just When I Need Him Most," by William C. Poole.

b) When you are tempted by your Enemy, what should you do?

____

____

2. 1 Peter 5:8; 2 Corinthians 11:14
   a) How does your Enemy sometimes appear?

____

____

   b) How can we discern the difference between the Enemy's guidance and the Holy Spirit's guidance?

____

____

3. James 1:2–4, 12–15
   a) In addition to the deceitful attacks by Satan, how do temptations arise?

____

____

   b) While God is never the author of temptation, He does permit us to be tested. What good can come out of temptations that you overcome?

____

____

B. Ephesians 6:10–18 says that we must put on the whole "armor" of God to have victory over Satan. What do the various pieces of the soldier's armor represent?
   a) Belt of ______________________________________

   b) Body armor of _________________________________

   c) Battle shoes of ________________________________

   d) Shield of ____________________________________

e) Helmet of ______________________________

f) Sword of ______________________________

Notice that the last piece of our spiritual armor (the sword) is an offensive weapon while all of the others are used for defense. Read Matthew 4:4, 7, and 10 to see how Jesus Christ used this "sword" when he was tempted. Describe the three spiritual attacks of Matthew 4 in your own words and paraphrase the Scripture passage that Jesus used to defeat each of them.

II. The spiritual battle plan

A. According to 1 John 3:8, why did the Son of God (Jesus Christ) come into our world?

____

____

B. According to James 4:7, when Satan attacks us,

1. What are we to do?

____

____

2. What will Satan do?

____

____

C. First Corinthians 10:13 describes four things we can be sure of when we are tempted. What are they?

1. ______________________________

2. ______________________________

3. ______________________________

4. ______________________________

III. Our ultimate victory

A. According to Hebrews 4:14,

1. Who is our great High Priest?

2. What does our High Priest do for us when we sin?

B. If we lose a battle to our Enemy (i.e., if we yield to temptation), is there any hope of recovery (1 John 2:1)?

C. What are we to do in that situation (1 John 1:9)?

(NOTE: The Greek New Testament word translated as "confess" literally means to "agree with God.")

D. How does Scripture describe a Christian who wins the spiritual battles of this world (1 John 5:5)? Praising God by faith for His forgiveness and faithfulness is a vital part of claiming the victory that is ours in Christ.

E. Rewrite Hebrews 4:15–16 in your own words:

F. According to Philippians 4:13,

1. Who will stand with us until we have victory over temptation?

2. Is there temptation that He cannot help us with?

G. Second Corinthians 2:11 warns us to be aware of the weapons and battle tactics that Satan might use against us. What do you think some of these weapons and tactics might be? Make a list:

H. Study Romans 8:35–39 and list the things that cannot separate us from the love of God in Christ Jesus:

I. Compare List G with List H. What do you observe?

J. Several scriptures indicate what you can do when you are tempted to sin against God:

1. Submit to God (James 4:7).
2. Learn to trust His grace for your weaknesses and needs (2 Cor 1:3–4).
3. Let the past be forgiven and gone when you have given it to Him (Phil 3:12–14).
4. Thank God that His grace is sufficient for you to have victory over temptation now (1 Thess 5:18).

Home Assignments

- Memorize the Key Verse (1 Cor 10:13).
- Read Genesis 3:1, 4–6 and Matthew 4:1–22. Apply their insights to your own struggles with temptation.

Step 3
Beginning to Grow

Key Verse

"But grow in the grace and knowledge of our Lord and Savior Jesus Christ."
—2 Peter 3:18

In our first lesson, we noted that when we become Christians, we become spiritual babies. We must grow and develop spiritually, much as a physical baby has to develop physically. In the physical world, the infant mortality rate is high. In many countries, children die for lack of medicine that would cost little. In the West, the infant mortality rate tends to be low, thanks to modern hospitals, doctors, and science. However, the rate of spiritual infant mortality is very great. Now let's see what we will need to do in order to grow up in our faith in Christ.

We see many other similarities between spiritual babies and physical babies, as well as some important differences. For example, an immature Christian is not able to digest the spiritual food that a mature Christian can take. This is why the apostle Paul draws a contrast between spiritual "milk" and spiritual "meat" (1 Cor 3:1–2). Do not become discouraged if you cannot understand all that you hear in a sermon or read from your Bible. At this early stage of your spiritual growth you will encounter many terms and ideas that are unfamiliar to you. That is okay. You are on a journey to discover more about the Christ life, so you will need to learn new things as you go along. In order to receive spiritual "meat" (the deeper teachings of the Holy Scriptures), you must first absorb the spiritual "milk" (easy-to-understand Bible truths).

On the other hand, unlike the physical development of a child, there is no uniform timetable for spiritual growth. We grow up spiritually as fast as we appropriate God's grace and knowledge, as fast as we practice obedience to the Lord. Someone who has been converted for only a short time may already be spiritually mature, while someone else may take years to mature spiritually.

If you are a parent, you can probably remember your children's uneven progress of physical maturation. When they were learning to walk, they stumbled and fell. They took one step at a time until they learned to walk across the room without falling. In the process of learning to walk independently, they received all kinds of bumps and bruises, but they did not stop trying to walk. We can expect the same thing to happen in our spiritual lives. In growing up spiritually, we will stumble and fall at times, and we may get bruises in the process, but we dare not quit walking in the light of Bible truth, both in our understanding and obedience.

Evangelist D. L. Moody illustrated this with a true story about his daughter. One winter evening he and his little girl bundled up and took a walk. The sidewalk was slick in spots, so he asked his daughter to let him take hold of her hand. She refused because she wanted to keep her hands in a new fur muff. As they were walking along, she slipped and fell. Her father helped her up and offered his hand to hold hers. Again she was hesitant, but this time she did grip one of his fingers. As they continued their walk, she once more lost her footing and fell harder than the first time. This time there were tears, and she asked her daddy to hold her hand tight. Moody said her experience illustrated how we must learn to put our complete trust and faith in God. For some of us, it takes a few more falls and bumps than for others, but even this is part of the spiritual growth process if we learn to hold tight to God's hand.

Bible Study

I. Necessity of spiritual growth

Growing in Christ includes fresh knowledge of what God has said in His Word and our heart's response of obedience to it.

A. Look up these Bible passages and respond in the blanks provided.

1. 2 Peter 1:3–4

   a) What gives us everything we need for an effective Christian life?

   ____

   ____

b) How does God expect us to receive His glory and excellence?

2. 2 Peter 1:5–7
   a) Use the following diagram to list the building blocks of Christian growth. (Begin from the bottom.)

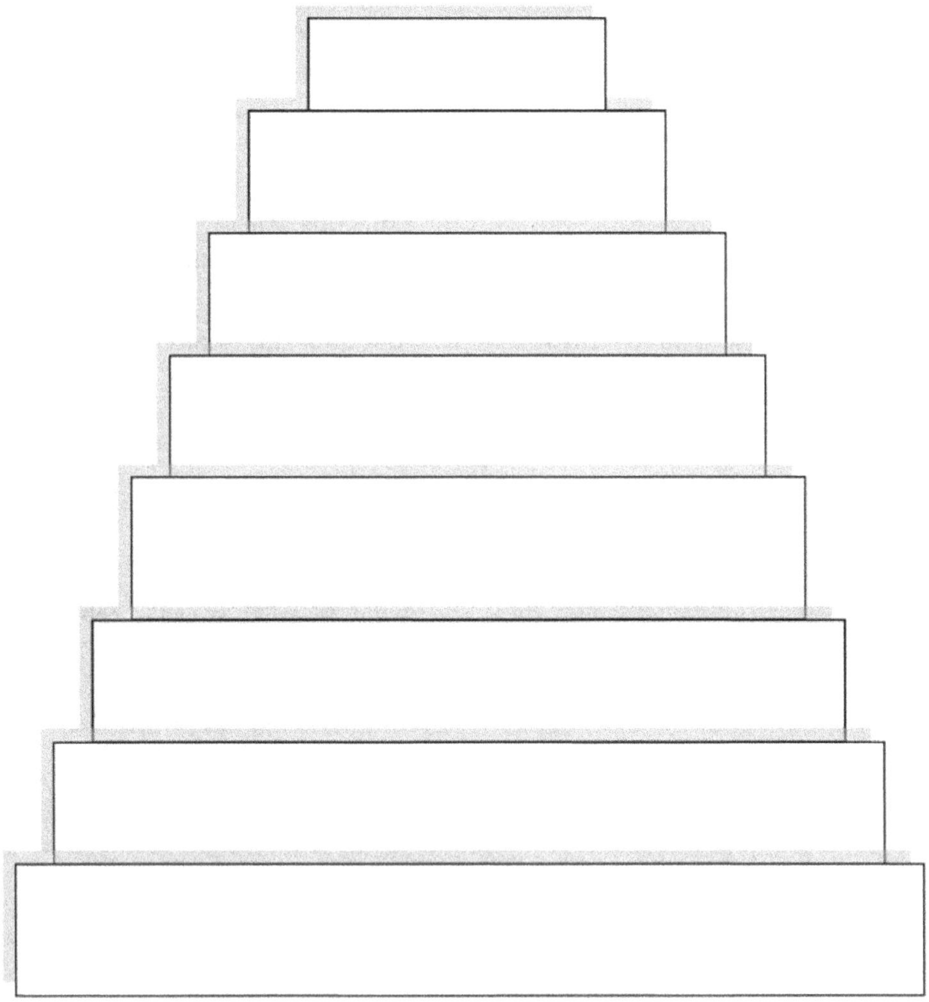

B. A well-built life

1. Read 2 Peter 1:8–11 and describe how your life will develop if you have these spiritual qualities in abundance.

2. Describe how your life will develop if you neglect these spiritual building blocks.

II. Beginning to grow

Study the following passages and summarize what they say we must do in order to grow in our faith.

1. 1 Peter 2:2–3

2. Ephesians 4:13–16

Home Assignments

- Memorize the Key Verse (2 Peter 3:18).
- Preview the Introduction to next week's lesson.

Step 4

Daily Disciplines

Key Verse

"Then Jesus said to His disciples, 'If anyone desires to come after Me, let him deny himself, and take up his cross, and follow Me.'" —Matthew 16:24

Introduction

A disciple is someone who lives a disciplined life. We do not discipline ourselves so that we may win favor with God. Rather, we train ourselves to respond to His call because we have already received His grace.

Jesus said, "Abide in Me, and I in you. As the branch cannot bear fruit by itself, unless it abides in the vine, neither can you, unless you abide in Me" (John 15:4). We bend our wills to the will of God through regular spiritual training (discipline). Our relationship with Him becomes deeper and more meaningful as we daily bend our wills to His good plan for our lives.

We live in an age of permissiveness with a lack of commitment on all levels of life, so it is harder for us to appreciate the need for any kind of discipline. Yet human beings could not exist without practicing certain disciplines every day. We must have self-control if we are to be healthy and live in healthy relationships with others. This is true of our relationship with God, just as it is of our relationships with other human beings.

When we commit our lives to Jesus Christ, we will take seriously His summons, "If anyone desires to come after Me, let him deny himself, and take up his cross daily, and follow Me" (Luke 9:23). Again, this does not mean that we have to do certain things to earn our salvation. We cannot buy eternal life.

That is God's gift to us. But if we are going to be optimally used of God, we need to discipline our lives so that we become stronger and more mature to face the tests that every Christ-follower will encounter. As the apostle Paul reminded his Christian friends, "It is God who works in you both to will and to do for His good pleasure" (Phil 2:13). Each decision we make by faith reconfirms and deepens the work of grace that God has already accomplished within us.

We might say that Paul's letters describe a life in which the Christian believer is working on the outside and God is working on the inside. One without the other is total failure. A person working out his own salvation by himself, apart from faith, is trying to lift himself by his own bootstraps—an effort that is doomed to failure (see Phil 2:12–13). Real discipline is not a vain effort to save ourselves. It is participating in the life-transforming work of God, who is our salvation.

What can you do to have more discipline in your life? For a start, train yourself to finish whatever you start, to be on time, and to fulfill the promises you make. These are just small beginnings, but important ones. It is like the athlete who trains his body to function the way it must if he is to reach his goals. He has to start slow, with simple exercises, then gradually work his way up to the more difficult and more strenuous levels of training.

Attend church regularly. Why? The church is your spiritual family, and you need the fellowship and encouragement of other believers. You need to have the Word of God explained to you. Think back to the baby who requires special food and care. That is what the church does for babies in Christ. It is the place to get spiritual food, biblical understanding, mutual encouragement, and a clear sense of direction for your life.

What are some other disciplines to which you believe God is calling you? Share these with other members of your discipleship group, who can help you evaluate them in the light of Scripture.

Bible Study

I. Disciplined living vs. unfocused living

A. Read the following Scripture passages and restate them in your own words.

1. Jeremiah 29:13

____

____

2. Titus 2:11–14

3. Romans 6:15–19

B. Hebrews 5:7–9 briefly describes the obedience of Jesus.

1. How did He learn obedience?

2. What do you suppose verse 9 means when it says our salvation depends on Jesus' obedience to His Father?

3. Why might someone fail to come to Christ if there's a lack of spiritual discipline and obedience in your life?

II. Training for the journey

A. In light of Philippians 1:6 and 2:8, how can discipline assist your spiritual journey and the life assignment God has given you?

B. Reflect on Hebrews 4:14–16. Write out what this text means to you at this point in your spiritual journey. It is very reassuring to know that when we fail, we can call on God and receive His help to get up and go again with a clean record (review 1 John 2:1).

C. Romans 15:1-6 declares that we are called not to please ourselves but to serve one another in love. How might God be calling you to serve other Christ-followers?

III. Developing mature characteristics

A. Read and reflect on Colossians 3:1–17 from a few different translations. In the two columns below, list the life characteristics that we are commanded to avoid and those we are encouraged to develop.

Characteristics to Avoid	Characteristics to Develop

Now circle two of the qualities that you need to develop. Ask God to show you where to begin. He will help you with your areas of need.

B. Having an accountability partner is important for a life of Christian discipleship. As you reflect on your needs and weaknesses, find someone of the same gender who could walk with you, pray with you, encourage you, speak the truth in love to you, and help you keep on track. Write that person's name here:

Home Assignments

- Memorize the Key Verse (Matt 16:24).
- Take some time each day to read and reflect on the Holy Scriptures.
- Ask someone to be your accountability partner for the rest of this course. Share with that person what you have already learned.

Step 5
Private Prayer

Key Verse

"So I say to you, ask, and it will be given to you; seek, and you will find; knock, and it will be opened to you." —Luke 11:9

Introduction

An effective Christian life is undergirded with dynamic prayer. Prayer is simply having honest, intimate conversation with God—both speaking and listening. As Richard C. Trench has so well stated, "Prayer is not overcoming God's reluctance; it is laying hold of His highest willingness."[1]

Prayer is a lifelong journey into the heart of God to seek His fellowship, His forgiveness, His guidance, and unraveling before Him all of our needs with confident faith in the One who seeks our highest and best. It is time invested with Him in a spirit of surrendered thanksgiving and praise.

Ours is the privilege of having holy conversation with all three members of the Holy Trinity. We sometimes make a great fuss over the style or words of our prayers, as well as the correct posture, thinking we must kneel or fold our hands together in order to pray. These are not essential to prayer at all. Prayer is simply talking with God and listening to Him, much as we would converse with someone else who is very important to us.

Use everyday language that your friends would understand rather than the language of the King James Bible. Talk with the Lord in a relaxed, confidential

1. As quoted in Frank S. Mead, *The Encyclopedia of Religious Quotations* (Westwood, NJ: Revell, 1965), 348.

way as if He were sitting or standing beside you—because He really is. Listen to God by reading portions from the Bible or Christian devotional books, listening to hymns and choruses, or simply being silent for a few minutes. This gives God opportunities to put His thoughts and plans into your mind.

You will help yourself if you make a special time for prayer each day. Your schedule may be so crowded that there seems to be no time left to do everything that's needed. But you will find time to do anything you really want to do. You will not be denying yourself too much.

Prayer and the study of God's Word are like eating and breathing for our inner lives. We need them to grow, keep fresh, and be vitally energized. God will honor a consistent prayer life. As you practice the discipline of daily prayer, you will grow as a Christ-follower, increasing in your joy and effectiveness for Him.

Bible Study

I. Movements of prayer illustrated by the Lord's Prayer (Matt 6:9–13)

A. Adoration and Praise to God (6:9): "Our Father in heaven, hallowed be Your name."

1. Many psalms express adoration, praise, and celebration of God (e.g., Pss 24; 33:1–7; 98; 100; 103; 104:1–34; 106:1–5; 148).

2. In this movement of prayer,
   a) Tell God that you are grateful for His love.
   b) Express your love for God and affirm your devotion to Him.
   c) Praise God for His majesty and His supreme qualities of love, justice, and righteousness.

B. Personal commitment to God and His cause (6:10): "Your kingdom come. Your will be done on earth as it is in heaven."

1. Examine Jesus' own declarations of commitment to His heavenly Father (Matt 7:24–27; Luke 22:39–46).

2. In this movement of prayer,
   a) Tell God that you will obey and follow Him whenever and wherever He calls you, to the best of your ability, regardless of the cost. This is

an essential part of embracing His senior partnership in your life.

b) Commit to God your life, your abilities, your time, your money, your influence, and everything else you have.

c) Ask God for more of His Spirit to strengthen you in keeping these commitments.

d) Identify definite steps that you will take to keep these commitments.

C. Petition and intercession (6:11): "Give us this day our daily bread."

1. As you tell God about your material needs and personal struggles, you can trust him to give you what He knows is best.

2. As you lift up needs of people in your circles of family, friends, neighbors, and co-workers, do not forget to pray for your enemies (Matt 5:43–46).

3. As you intercede for others,

   a) Seek to feel their pain, their lostness, and the weight of their burdens.

   b) With prayer, bring the love and grace of God into their situations.

   c) Expect God to touch their specific needs. (See Mark 11:22–24; James 1:5–8; Heb 5:7–9; Eph 6:18–19; 1 Tim 2:1–4.)

   d) In faith, imagine them responding affirmatively to God's love.

D. Confession and forgiveness (6:12): "And forgive us our debts, as we also forgive our debtors."[2]

1. Many scriptures speak of the spirit of forgiveness that should characterize God's people. (See Matt 6:12, 14, 15; 5:21–26; Mark 11:25–26; Prov 28:13; Ps 106:6–7; Ps 51:1–17; James 5:16; 1 John 1:9).

2. In this movement of prayer,

   a) If you are angry, resentful, or lustful—or if you harbor any other ungodly attitude—confess it and ask God to guard your heart from it (see Prov 4:23).

   b) If you have been disobedient to God, confess specifically how you have disobeyed Him.

   c) Forgive yourself for what you have done.

2. Some translations say "trespasses" instead of "debts." Luke's account of the Lord's Prayer says "sins" instead of "debts" or "trespasses."

d) If others have harmed you, forgive them.

e) Accept God's cleansing of your sin and the sins of others.

f) Commit yourself to make restitution to anyone you have slighted, hurt, or harmed, whenever that is possible..

E. Petition for God's guidance (6:13a): "And do not lead us into temptation, but deliver us from the evil one."

1. James 1:5–8 instructs us to ask the Lord for wisdom in our daily decisions. He is eager to give us insight into every choice that we make.
2. Notice the striking contrast between the first half of John 10:10 ("The thief does not come except to steal, and to kill, and to destroy.") and the last half ("I have come that they may have life, and that they may have it more abundantly.") In this movement of prayer,
   a) Ask the Lord to counsel you in every decision, so that you may enjoy His abundant blessings.
   b) Ask Him to help you avoid doing anything that would lead you into spiritual or material trouble. (Note the stories in Joshua 9:1–18 and Matthew 2:1–18.)

F. Praise and thanksgiving (6:13b): "For Yours is the kingdom and the power and the glory forever. Amen."

1. Many Scripture passages can stimulate this spirit within us. (See Pss 100:4–5; 34:1–8; Phil 3:1a; 4:4; Col 2:6–7; 4:2; 1 Thess 5:18.)
2. In this movement of prayer,
   a) Thank God for your salvation, spiritual victory, and purpose in life.
   b) Thank Him for His daily guidance and answers to prayer.

II. Qualities of effective prayer[3]

A. Availability

1. Prayer should be a regular, planned activity of our daily lives. Reflect on the prayer life of Jesus described in Luke 4:42; 9:18a; 11:1; and 22:39–42. What do these passages teach you about how to conduct your own prayer life?

____

____

3. The following ideas were inspired by the writings of William Parker and Elaine St. John in *Prayer Can Change Your Life*.

2. Jesus tells a parable about an unjust judge who was reluctant to heed the pleas of a desperate woman but finally relented (Luke 18:1–8). (This is not a story of comparison, but one of contrast.) What do you learn from this story that would help you respond to people who seek your help?

____

____

B. Submissiveness

1. What do the following verses teach you about having a submissive spirit in prayer?
   a) 1 John 3:21–22

   ____

   ____

   b) John 15:7

   ____

   ____

   c) 1 John 5:14–15

   ____

   ____

   d) Psalm 37:5

   ____

   ____

C. Affirmation

1. When we claim God’s promises in prayer, we place ourselves in a position opposite to that of unbelief. The world says, “Seeing is believing,” but a Christ-follower believes in order to see. As Jesus told Martha at the tomb of her brother Lazarus, “Did I not say to you that if you would believe you would see the glory of God?” (John 11:40).

2. Reflect on the following Bible verses and record your thoughts about affirming faith.
   a) Hebrews 11:6

   ____

   ____

   b) James 5:13–18

   ____

   ____

   c) Matthew 21:22 (parallel: Mark 11:24)

   ____

   ____

   d) James 1:6–8

   ____

   ____

   e) Hebrews 10:22–23

   ____

   ____

   f) Mark 9:23–24

   ____

   ____

Prayers where we claim and affirm the promises made to us in Holy Scripture empower the Lord to give Himself more fully to us.

D. Attentiveness

1. Effective prayer is open, expectant, quiet, and trusting. Christ-followers who pray in a spirit of active listening will wait open-heartedly for God's answer. Read these two biblical examples of attentive prayer and note how you might apply them to your own prayer life:

   a) 1 Samuel 3:1–10

   ____

   ____

   b) Luke 22:29–46

   ____

   ____

Home Assignments

- Memorize the Key Verse (Luke 11:9).
- Talk with your accountability partner about any challenges you face in having a time of daily private prayer.

Step 6:

Deepening Your Prayer Life

Key Verse

"If you abide in Me, and My words abide in you, you will ask what you desire, and it shall be done for you." —John 15:7

Introduction:

This second lesson on prayer is designed to explore some additional aspects of your prayer life. Prayer is the most important spiritual discipline that a Christ-follower can practice, so we encourage you to deepen your prayer life throughout your discipleship journey.

Expect the Holy Spirit to pray uniquely through your personality, so do not try to pray just like someone else. If you try to imitate your pastor or a Christian friend, your prayer will be just that—an imitation. You need the real thing. Make it your aim to be totally natural, utterly sincere, and completely yielded to the Holy Spirit.

At mealtime offer prayers of thanks and bring your family needs to God. This can be a significant time of bonding with other members of your family, your common declaration of dependence on the Lord. It is helpful to have other prayer times with your family members, individually and as a group. Make them short and meaningful. You might set aside some time in the evening to share the best things that happened to family members during the day so that you can celebrate together, support one another, and lift each other up as members of a Christian family.

Notice how prayers are used in public worship. Here are some traditional types of public prayer, although you may find that some of them are not used in your congregation's worship services:

Invocation. This is not an invitation for God to be present in the service, because He is everywhere present. Instead, this brief prayer at the beginning of corporate worship acknowledges that God is there and expresses our openness to Him during the time of worship.

Pastoral Prayer. In this prayer, the pastor expresses your corporate adoration, praise, confession, commitment, and petitions for God's intercession in specific needs of the congregation and far beyond. While other people may be asked to offer this prayer, a member of the pastoral staff is usually best acquainted with the needs of the congregation.

Prayers at a Public Altar. In some congregations, people will be invited to come to a public altar (kneeling bench) to pray for salvation, rededication of one's life, consecration to receive the Holy Spirit's fullness, divine healing, divine guidance for specific problems, or to invite corporate intervention for specific needs.

Benediction. This is a pronouncement of God's blessing upon the people as they disperse. Some would say it is not technically a prayer because it is not addressed *to* God but to God's people *on His behalf.*

At the end of this session's Bible Study, we will think about ways we can pray on the basis of what God has said in His Word. By praying Scripture, we can claim God's promises, celebrate His presence in hard times, and learn how to pray for others whose burdens we share. Scripture praying can be a rich experience, as you'll see.

Bible Study

I. New Testament prayer

A. Read the following Scripture passages in which Jesus instructs His disciples about the purpose and spirit of prayer. Then paraphrase each passage in your own words.

1. Luke 18:1

____

____

2. John 14:13; 16:23

____

____

3. John 16:24

____

____

4. Matthew 6:6

____

____

B. According to these Scripture passages, what are some of the conditions for effective prayer?

1. 1 Peter 3:12

____

____

2. 1 John 3:21–23

____

____

3. 1 John 5:14–15

____

____

4. Philippians 4:6

____

____

C. According to these verses, what are some things we should ask for ourselves when we pray?

1. James 1:5

____

____

2. Acts 4:29–30

____

____

3. Psalm 119:18

____

____

4. Psalm 119:133

____

____

5. Psalm 19:14

____

____

6. Psalm 34:4

____

____

II. Praying the Scriptures

A. When we pray scriptures, we claim God's promise when He said, "I am alert and active, watching over My word to perform it" (Jer 1:12 AB). Romans 10:17 says that "faith comes by hearing, and hearing by the word of God." So praying scriptures will allow faith to enter our hearts and minds, dispelling our fear and anxiety. We can pray many prayers that come directly out of biblical material. Here are a few examples:

1. *For Assurance.* "Lord, we thank You for the wonderful promise You have given us in Matthew 28:20, 'Lo, I am with you always.' In this time of

trouble, we thank You for the sure knowledge that You are here with us and that we do not need to face this alone…"

2. *For Peace.* "Father, the situation today is troubling, so we claim the peace that You promised us in John 14:27, when You said, 'Peace I leave with you, My peace I give to you; not as the world gives do I give to you. Let not your heart be troubled, neither let it be afraid.' Let us sense Your peace right now."

3. *For Relief from Anxiety.* "Lord, the apostle Paul tells us in Philippians 4:6–7, 'Don't worry about anything; instead, pray about everything. Tell God what you need, and thank him for all he has done. Then you will experience God's peace, which exceeds anything we can understand. His peace will guard our hearts and minds as we live in Christ Jesus' (NLT). We confess that we're worried about ____________, but we turn it over to You now. We thank You in advance for taking care of it, and we ask You to guard our hearts and minds from any further anxiety about it."

4. *For Wisdom.* "Lord, Your Word says in James 1:5 that if we lack wisdom in anything, we should ask You. Today, we're in a difficult situation and don't know what to do about it. We need to decide what to do about __________________, and we are confident that You will reveal what we should do. We thank You for giving us Your guidance, Lord, and praise You for being our wisdom."

5. *For Disciplining a Rebellious Child.* "Heavenly Father, we have come up against a difficult problem with [name of child], and we do not know what to do. You gave us this child, and we want with all our hearts to raise this child "in the training and admonition of the Lord," as Ephesians 6:4 tells us to do. But what we have done to provide guidance and discipline is not working, so we come to You. We ask You for the wisdom and strength to fulfill this command of Your Word."

6. *For Courage in Adversity.* "Lord, You promised in Matthew 7:24 that anyone who hears Your Word and puts it into practice is like a man who builds his house on a rock. You said that when the rains come and the floods rise and the winds beat against his house, it will not fall because it is built on a solid foundation. Well, Lord, we're in a real storm right now, and we need courage to face ______________. I pray that You will hold us steady in the storm. Keep our faith strong and sure. Remind

us that You are our unmovable Rock and You will be our victory in this situation."

7. *For Overcoming Temptation.* "Heavenly Father, this week I let my mind wander into paths which are neither healthy nor wise. You tell me that I am to bring every thought captive and make it obey Christ (2 Cor 10:5), so I claim Your cleansing and Your power to bring all of my thoughts and desires under Your lordship."

8. *For Spiritual Examination.* "Father, the psalmist David said, "Search me, O God, and know my heart; test me and know my anxious thoughts. See if there is any offensive way in me, and lead me in the way everlasting" (Ps 139:23–24 NIV1984). Lord, I want my heart to be pure and my mind and my life to be filled with Your Spirit and Your thoughts. I wait quietly here with my heart open and listening. Say anything to me that You have to say, and I will listen and respond."

9. *For Children's Sleep.* "Lord, You have promised in Isaiah 54:13, 'All your children *shall* be taught by the LORD, and great *shall be* the peace of your children.' So I ask You to watch over [child's name] tonight. Give [him or her] a peaceful night of sleep, and help [him or her] to learn more about You every day."

B. Keep a Scripture prayer notebook organized by topics, such as healing, salvation, material needs, children, marriage, work, and so on. As you find a scripture promise that fits a particular need, write it in the appropriate section of your notebook. When you or a friend has a need, you'll have scriptures at your fingertips to pray over the situation.

C. Some Internet websites list scripture prayers as well, including www.prayingscriptures.com and www.believers.org/believe/bel117.htm.

D. One surprising benefit of praying the Scriptures is that they become embedded in our hearts and minds, and they rise up to comfort us in time of need. This is a much easier method of scripture recall than traditional memorization.

Home Assignments

- Memorize the Key Verse (John 15:7).
- Meet with your accountability partner and offer some scripture prayers for specific needs that are on your heart.

Step 7
Read the Bible Devotionally

Key Verse
"As Your words are taught, they give light; even the simple can understand them." —Psalm 119:130 NLT

Introduction
The Bible is both a divine and human book. The men who wrote were guided by God's Holy Spirit. Using their unique experiences and personalities, these godly people wrote the sixty-six books that were gathered into the book we now call the Bible.

So the Bible is the inspired Word of God. It records God's creation of the universe, and the ultimate destiny of humanity. Its central person is Jesus Christ, and its central message is eternal life, how to have it, and how to live with hope, regardless of life's circumstances.

The Bible comprises two major sections: the Old Testament and New Testament, so called because they were written before and after the birth of Christ, who established the new covenant (testament) of God's love. The Old Testament contains these thirty-nine books divided into five categories:

Law: Genesis–Deuteronomy
History: Joshua–Esther
Wisdom Literature: Job–Song of Solomon
Major Prophets: Isaiah–Daniel
Minor Prophets: Hosea–Malachi

The New Testament consists of these twenty-seven books, also divided into five categories:

Gospels: Matthew, Mark, Luke, and John
Beginning of the Church: Acts
Paul's Letters: Romans–Philemon
General Letters: Hebrews–Jude
Prophecy: Revelation

Notice the various kinds of literature contained in the Bible. We need to be aware of the type of book we are reading whenever we delve into the Bible, because that will affect the way we interpret what we read. For example, a book of history and a book of poetry may describe the same event in very different ways, so we should be aware of those differences.

There are a variety of ways to study the Bible, but in this session we will focus on studying the Bible as part of your devotional life.[1] Here are some practical guidelines for making the most of your devotional Bible study.

Read regularly. Just as we must eat nourishing food regularly for the good of our body, we must read the Bible regularly for the good of our inner life. To make sure this happens, it's best to set aside a definite time of day for reading the Bible. You are the only one who can say what time of day is best for you, and you may have to change that time occasionally to fit your circumstances. Yet, unless you have a daily pattern of Bible study, your reading will be spasmodic and disappointing.

Read selectively. Unless you already have an excellent knowledge of the Bible, you should read according to some set plan. If you skip here and there to read wherever the Bible opens, you will soon tire of Bible reading and decide that you are not growing from it. What are some plans you might follow?

a. *The entire Bible in a year.* There are many plans for reading the Bible through in a year.[2] However, this can be a daunting challenge, especially for a new Christian.

b. *A Bible book.* Choose a book of the Bible that interests you and read one chapter a day. Each new day, pick up where you ended the previous day.

---

1. The following material has been adapted from *Let's Study the Bible,* by Kenneth E. Jones. (Used by permission.)
2. See Jerry A. Hickson, *God's Word for Me* (Anderson, IN: Warner Press, 2011), which provides six tracks for reading through the Bible in a year.

c. *Lives of Bible men or women.* If you enjoy reading the biographies of great people, trace the lives of important men or women of the Bible. A Bible dictionary will help you locate the passages that tell a person's story from beginning to end.

d. *Topical studies.* Use a Bible concordance to find passages by various Bible writers on a particular topic, such as *grace, humility, love, comfort, sanctification, peace,* or any other word you might choose.

No matter what plan you choose, read regularly from the Psalms and Proverbs, and spend much of your time in the Gospels. (It is not by accident that these four books are placed at the beginning of the New Testament. They were not written first, but these accounts of Jesus' life are the basis for understanding of the rest of it.)

Read expectantly. As you read the Bible, expect God to speak to you. You may want to begin your Bible study time with prayer, saying, "Lord, speak to my heart. I need to hear from You today." If you expect Him to give the spiritual nourishment you need, He will not disappoint you.

Read prayerfully. Bible reading itself is a form of prayer, for it is communion with God. So when you read the Bible, place yourself in a prayerful frame of mind, asking God for wisdom and understanding.

Read obediently. Obedience is essential to meaningful Bible reading. While simple reading can give you an intellectual knowledge of God's will for you, only your obedience will reveal the significance of His commands. Through obedience to God's Word, the Word becomes an integral part of your life. Then you will be truly Christlike.

Bible Study

I. The importance of Scripture

A. Reflect on the following verses and restate them in your own words.

1. 2 Peter 1:21

____

____

2. 2 Timothy 3:16–17

____

____

3. Psalm 19:7–12

____

____

B. Invest some time in reading Psalm 119, the longest chapter of the Bible. The psalmist gives many reasons for reading and reflecting on Scripture. List some of them

____

____

____

____

II. Promises to claim

A. The Bible makes hundreds of specific promises of blessing to everyone who obeys God and fully trusts Him. Here are a few examples:

1. "The righteous person faces many troubles, but the LORD comes to the rescue each time." (Ps 34:19 NLT)

2. "Anything is possible if a person believes." (Mark 9:23 NLT)

3. "Anyone who believes in God's Son has eternal life" (John 3:36 NLT).

4. "Give all your worries and cares to God, for he cares about you." (1 Peter 5:7 NLT)

5. "Here on earth you will have many trials and sorrows. But take heart, because I have overcome the world." (John 16:33 NLT)

6. "My grace is all you need. My power works best in weakness." (2 Cor 12:9 NLT)

B. Write here some other promises that you find as you read the Bible.

____

____

Home Assignments

- Memorize the Key Verse (Ps 119:130).
- Ask your accountability partner to contact you every day this week to make sure you keep your daily Bible study time.

Step 8

In-Depth Bible Study

Key Verse

"Your word I have hidden in my heart, that I might not sin against You."
—Psalm 119:11

Introduction

Last week, we considered Bible study as a part of your daily devotional practice. How are you doing? This week, we begin more in-depth Bible study. This lesson describes a method you can use to deepen your investigation of the Bible and explores some reference books you can use to expand the horizons of your Bible study.

Let's start with the method. Here are some questions you can use to dig deeper into the meaning of any Scripture passage. (You will have an opportunity to try this in our "Bible Study" section for this week.)

1. What does this passage say? What does it literally mean if you "take it at face value"?
2. What did it mean to the person(s) who originally read it? (This will take a bit of research with the reference books we will introduce later in this lesson. You want to find out: Who wrote it? To whom was it written? Where was it written? What was the political, social, cultural, and religious climate at the time?) Working through this question is critically important for a proper biblical understanding.

3. What was the occasion? In other words, was this passage written to answer a particular question, solve a problem, issue a warning, or make a promise? What seems to have been the writer's purpose?
4. What is the timeless truth of this passage? What does it say to any generation, at any time, in any place in the world? (Write this down in your own words, using no more than two or three sentences.)
5. What significance does it have for Christ-followers today, given the current state of our world?
6. What significance does it have for you? What do you see in the passage that ought to affect your relationship toward God? How you feel about yourself? How you respond to others?
7. If you took seriously what this passage says, what action(s) should you take this week? What action(s) should you avoid?
8. How does the message of this Scripture passage stack up with other Bible passages you have studied?

We have a great variety of Bible reference books to help us dig deeper into the meaning of Scripture. We are blessed to live in a day when many of these resources have become available on the Internet at little or no cost. Here are basic Bible reference tools that you can use for in-depth Bible study early in your Christian walk:

Concordance. This is like a topical dictionary of Bible passages. It lists most (or all) Bible verses where a particular word or phrase appears. Use a concordance to find Bible verses that refer to a subject you may be thinking about.

Topical Concordance. Unlike a regular Bible concordance, the topical concordance lists verses that speak about the topic, even if that particular word is not found in the passage. This tool may also be called a Topical Bible.

Bible Dictionary. While a regular dictionary gives you the definition of a word, a Bible dictionary gives information about Bible topics, geographical features, personalities, and much more.

Bible Commentary. A commentary gives you extended comments about a passage you are studying. It may provide information about archaeological finds, linguistic studies, and other modern research that sheds light on the passage. However, commentaries also speculate about the meaning of each passage, and not all commentaries are of the same theological value. Seek the advice of a more mature Bible student, such as your accountability partner, as you decide which commentaries you might use.

Bible Atlas. Your Bible may already have a few maps that show where key biblical events occurred. A Bible atlas is a more comprehensive collection of maps, showing how the Holy Land looked at different times in history. It may also give information about the climate and political alliances of various regions mentioned in the Bible.

Gospel Parallel. This book lists passages from each of the Synoptic Gospels (Matthew, Mark, and Luke) that describe a particular event or teaching from Jesus' ministry, so you can compare them to each other. You will find some fascinating differences and similarities between them.

It's also helpful to consult different translations of the passage you are studying for additional insights. Internet websites such as www.biblegateway.com and www.crosswalk.com allow you to make these comparisons online.

> **"It ain't those parts of the Bible that I can't understand that bother me, it is the parts that I do understand."**
> **— Mark Twain**

Bible Study

I. Two in-depth Bible studies

A. Read 2 Timothy 2:14–15 and answer the following questions:

1. What does this passage say?

____

____

2. What did it mean to the person(s) who originally read it?
   a) Who wrote it?
   b) To whom was it written?
   c) Where was it written?
   d) What was the political, social, cultural, and religious climate at the time?

3. What was the occasion? What seems to have been the writer's purpose?

____

____

4. What is the timeless truth of this passage? (Write this down in your own words, using no more than two or three sentences.)

____

____

5. What significance does it have for Christ-followers today, given the current state of our world?

____

____

6. What significance does it have for you? What do you see in the passage that ought to affect your relationship toward God? How you feel about yourself? How you respond to others?

____

____

7. If you took seriously what this passage says, what action(s) should you take this week? What action(s) should you avoid?

____

____

8. How does the message of this Scripture passage stack up with other Bible passages you have studied?

____

____

B. Read and apply the same study questions to Colossians 3:15–17.

____

____

II. Scripture memorization

Scripture memorization will help you stay focused in times of weakness and temptation. Use these techniques to improve your ability to memorize scriptures:

1. Think through the meaning of the verse (or passage).
2. Apply the verse personally. (How do you need this truth in your own life?)
3. Say the verse out loud several times or, if appropriate, pray it out loud.
4. Write the verse a few times.
5. Repeat the reference before and after you say the verse.
6. Check your Bible periodically to be sure you are recalling the text word-perfect.
7. Use the verses in your daily meditation and share it with others.
8. Review verses you have learned at least once each day. (This is the real secret of long-term retention.)
9. Learn two new verses each week. (This will increase your capacity to memorize.)

Home Assignments

- Memorize the Key Verse (Psalm 119:11).
- Select one or more of the following passages for an in-depth Bible study this week, using the questions on pages 42–43 in this workbook:

  - John 10:11–18
  - John 15:1–8
  - Romans 8:35–39
  - 1 Corinthians 15:50–57
  - James 1:22–25

Step 9
Keeping the Ordinances

Key Verse

"If you know these things, blessed are you if you do them." —John 13:17

Introduction

An *ordinance* is a Christian ritual commanded by Jesus Christ Himself. This symbolic act helps us remember an essential truth taught by Jesus, it bears testimony to others (both believers and unbelievers) of our commitment to the Lord, and it deepens the intimacy of our relationship with other Christ-followers who share the ordinance with us.

Christian ordinances are to be observed by the universal church throughout the ages. This is true of only three rituals: baptism, communion (or the Lord's Supper), and footwashing. Each of these symbolic acts represents a great spiritual truth or experience that Jesus instructed us to remember. Let us consider the biblical basis for each of these practices.

Baptism

The first command that Jesus gave His disciples after His resurrection was: "Therefore go and make disciples of all nations, baptizing them in the name of the Father and of the Son and of the Holy Spirit, and teaching them to obey everything I have commanded you" (Matt 28:19–20 NIV1984). Why would Christ expect His disciples to be baptized?

Baptism does not wash away our sin; only the shed blood of Jesus can do that. However, baptism is the symbol of our being washed clean from our sins to begin a whole new way of life as a Christ-follower. The Greek word for baptize is *baptō*, which means "to dip" or "submerge,"[1] so Christian baptism is the ritual submersion of a believer in water.

Historically, baptism speaks of Christ's death, burial, and resurrection. Symbolically, it testifies that the Christ-follower has died to sin, so that the "old life" has been buried and the believer has "risen" to walk in newness of life. Prophetically, baptism proclaims that if the Lord delays His coming until after the believer dies, the believer's body will be buried but will rise again when Christ returns.

In being baptized, you give a public testimony to your acceptance of Jesus Christ as Savior and Lord. Baptism is an outward symbol of an inward work already performed in your heart by the Lord Jesus. By being baptized, you show the world that you identify yourself with Christ in obedience to His Word.

The New Testament shows that people were baptized very soon after committing their lives to Christ. If you have not already been baptized, you will be given the opportunity soon. Follow the Lord in baptism, and you will experience the joy of obedience to what He has commanded in His Word.

Bible Study

I. Why baptism is an ordinance

A. Jesus Himself was baptized (Matt 3:13–17) and commanded that every believer be baptized (Matt 28:19).

B. The apostles continued it (Acts 2:38, 41; 8:26–38).

C. This immersion in water symbolizes our death to sin and our resurrection to new life in Christ (Rom 6:1–5).

II. New Testament teachings about baptism

A. Why was Jesus baptized (Matt 3:13–17)?

____

____

1. W. E. Vine, *Expository Dictionary of New Testament Words* (Westwood, NJ: Revell, 1967, 6).

B. Who is an appropriate candidate for Christian baptism (Rom 6:3–5)?

____

____

C. Why is the ritual of baptism not appropriate before conversion (Matt 28:19–20; Acts 8:36–39)?

____

____

D. How soon should a believer be baptized after conversion to Jesus Christ (Acts 16:29–34)?

____

____

Communion

Communion (or the Lord's Supper) is a symbolic meal for believers, consisting of bread and grape juice.[2] First Corinthians 11:23–26 says that when we take the Lord's Supper, we share with Christ-followers everywhere the meaning of Christ's death on the cross. Verse 26 says that as often as we share the bread and the cup in Communion, we proclaim the Lord's death until He comes.

Verse 27 of this text says that we ought to partake of the Lord's Supper with self-examination, remembering that we are not worthy to have fellowship with God because of our sins, but Christ's death entitles us to a place at the table. So Communion is a time of close fellowship between Christ and you, as well as with all Christ-followers.

Most Protestant congregations practice open communion, that is, allowing Christ-followers from any congregation or church group to participate. We believe that the table of Communion is open to every person who has accepted Christ as Savior and Lord.

Some congregations take Communion every Sunday; others, one Sunday each month; and others, less frequently. Jesus instructed us to share in Communion to remind us of His death until He comes again, but He did not prescribe a certain time or frequency for taking Communion.

2. Jesus first shared Communion with His twelve disciples at the end of a Jewish Passover meal, so He used the unleavened bread and wine of Passover. Early Christians continued to use unleavened bread and wine for Communion, and many believers still do. However, leavened bread and grape juice are now used in many Protestant Communion services, which reminds us that Communion represents our new covenant with Christ, not the old covenant of Passover.

Bible Study

I. Why Communion is an ordinance

A. Jesus instituted it (Luke 22:14–20; Matt 26:26–29).

B. He challenged us to continue it as a memorial of His death (Luke 22:19–20).

C. The apostles continued it (Acts 2:42; 1 Cor 11:23–26).

II. New Testament teachings about Communion

A. What spiritual benefits do you receive by taking Communion (Luke 22:14–20)?

____

____

B. What should be our attitude when we take Communion (1 Cor 11:23–26)?

____

____

Footwashing

The ritual washing of feet, though clearly taught in John 13, is not practiced by many Christians in our time. Few believers would deny that this ordinance is biblical or that Christ commanded His followers to observe it, but some feel that it is too undignified or distasteful for a worship service. Yet Jesus commanded us to wash one another's feet to remind us that we are called to be humble servants of one another, not proud persons who lord it over each other.

Believers who participate in a service of footwashing often become strong proponents of it because it is a tender time of mutual submission and grace for those who participate. Men and women usually go to separate rooms for this celebration. They may sing choruses, share testimonies, and express appreciation to one another as they wash each other's feet. Occasionally, husbands and wives will wash each other's feet. This, too, is a sweet time in the Lord.

Bible Study

I. Why footwashing is an ordinance

A. Jesus instituted it to teach servanthood and humility (John 13:1–17).

B. The apostles continued it (1 Tim 5:10).

C. Every Christian is blessed by observing it (John 13:17).

II. New Testament teachings about footwashing

A. Read reflectively John 13:12–17. What do you see in this ordinance that would contribute to a happy, fulfilled life in Christ?

B. Read Romans 13:8. The Greek word translated as "owe" in this verse is translated as "ought" in Jesus' command to wash one another's feet (John 13:14). How does keeping the ordinance (John 13) demonstrate the spirit of Romans 13?

Summary

All three ordinances teach us important truths about our relationship to God and to one another. Baptism illustrates our new relationship with Jesus Christ Himself, saying that we have been "born again" in Christ. Communion points to our relationship with God the Father by virtue of Christ's cross. It says that we are saved from condemnation for our sins through Christ's shed blood. Footwashing points to our relationship with one another as family members in Christ. It declares that we serve one another in love, as Christ commanded us.

Home Assignments

- Memorize the Key Verse (John 13:17).
- Share with your accountability partner a meaningful experience you have had with a Christian ordinance.
- Discuss with your partner this hymn by D. S. Warner, which is sometimes sung at ordinance services:

By Your blessed Word obeying,
Lord, we prove our love sincere;
For we hear You gently saying,
"Love will do as well as hear."

Chorus
Dear Redeemer, we would hallow
All Your Word, so firm and true,
In Your footsteps meekly follow;
Your commands we love to do.

In Your wisdom, Lord, confiding
We will follow in Your way;
With Your love in us abiding
'Tis delightful to obey.

Each commandment You have given
Is a way-mark on the road
Leading up from earth to heaven
To the blessed throne of God.[3]

3. D. S. Warner, "By Your Blessed Word Obeying." *Worship the Lord: Hymnal of the Church of God* (Anderson, IN: Warner Press, 1989), no. 348

Step 10

Stewardship of Money

Key Verse

"Ascribe to the Lord the glory due his name; bring an offering and come into his courts." —Psalm 96:8 NIV1984

Introduction

As we've seen, spiritual growth is God's plan for you as a Christian. Stewardship is an important part of that growth. So what is stewardship? Christian stewardship is the practical acknowledgment that God owns everything, and I am to be a faithful manager of all that He has given to me. Stewardship includes at least three key areas of my life: my time, my talent, and my treasure.

How we view our possessions will determine how we use them, so we must answer this primary question: Who really owns what I possess? In other words, do I own my possessions, or does God? If God owns them all, then I have the privilege and responsibility of managing them well for Him.

Tithing is one way to acknowledge God's ownership of our possessions. Tithing is taught in both the Old and New Testaments. *Tithe* literally means a "tenth." By giving God the first tenth of any financial income we receive (the "first fruits" of our labors), we acknowledge that He owns all of it.

Here are some tithing facts to ponder:

1. When we choose to tithe, we exercise our faith in God. We trust God to take care of our financial needs.

2. In both the Old and New Testaments, God directed His people to support financially the ministries He instituted. (We will explore this further in this week's Bible Study.)
3. When we do not tithe, the Enemy of our souls has a way of devouring the resources we keep so that we find ourselves sliding into debt.
4. Christ-followers who tithe often discover that they live on the remaining 90 percent better than they were able to live on the 100 percent.

Some new Christ-followers ask, Why should we give to the church? Why not tithe to other good causes instead?

This week's Bible Study shows that God calls us to give a tithe to our local house of worship. If you are not deeply involved in the life of your congregation at this point, you may not realize all that it does, so let's take a moment to consider this. Jesus Christ established the church for many reasons: to spread the good news of salvation, to disciple believers, to provide fellowship and encouragement, to care for those who are suffering and in pain, and to care for those in need of life's basic necessities (such as widows and orphans). We enjoy the benefits of our Christian faith because other believers provided the resources for these essential ministries. Money provides places of worship, ministers' salaries, Christian literature and broadcasts, and other methods of spreading the good news around the world. Our faithful giving continues the work of Jesus Christ and the proclamation of His gospel.

Another question we, as growing believers, will want to explore is, How can I increase my giving beyond a tithe? Make sure you use all available means to promote systematic, proportionate giving. Offering envelopes and online bank transfers are two easy ways to be faithful in giving. Watch for opportunities to give special offerings for missions projects, radio ministries, and other outreach programs that your congregation supports. Your church may also sponsor a faith promise emphasis each year. Faith promise events challenge you to pledge a certain amount of money to the work of the church, even though you do not know where it will come from, and you trust the Lord to provide that gift through some sort of windfall during the year. Christians who participate in faith promise have amazing stories of how God has blessed them "exceedingly abundantly above" anything they have known before, so they could give the additional gift they had pledged (Eph 3:20).

Bible Study

I. The Old Testament establishes tithing as a basic principle of God's plan for financing His work.

A. Leviticus 27:30 and 33 say that the tithe (one-tenth) is "holy to the Lord." The word *holy* literally means "set apart" for God's purpose alone. Why do you think a tithe is to be altogether set apart for Him?

B. Read about Jacob's vow in Genesis 28:20–22. What did he promise to do, and why do you think he promised this?

C. Deuteronomy 26:1–15 commands God's people to give the "first fruits" of their harvests to God. Why do you suppose we are not commanded to give God our surplus (i.e., anything we don't need) instead?

You can give without loving,
but you can never love without giving.
— Victor Hugo

II. The New Testament says that generous giving expresses our gratitude for God's love.

A. John 3:16 expresses the generous spirit of God in sending His Son to die for our sins. How does this affect your desire to give something back to God?

____

____

B. Reflect on Matthew 6:1–4 and summarize its meaning. When we give to God's kingdom in a right spirit, what will He do?

____

____

C. What does Luke 6:38 say about being generous in our giving?

____

____

D. What are two key concepts about giving in 1 Corinthians 16:2?

____

____

E. Reflect on 2 Corinthians 9:6–7. What giving principle is taught here?

____

____

F. How is generous giving an expression of trusting faith (2 Corinthians 9:8)?

____

____

G. List some of the principles for Christian giving noted in 2 Corinthians 8:1–12.

____

____

____

____

H. How would you apply the promise of Philippians 4:18–19 to tithing?

____

____

III. Guidelines for Christian Financial Freedom

The list below was part of a discussion in a class for Christian leaders. How do you react to these guidelines in light of our study of God's plan for us to live abundantly? If you would change some of these, how would you change them—and why?

1. I understanding that all possessions—income, investments, talents, and time—are not ours but are given to us by God to use and invest for His kingdom's sake.

2. Tithe 10 percent to the Lord out of the first part of our **gross income**.

3. Set long-term and short-term goals for ourselves and our families: Spiritual growth goals, goals for financial freedom, plans for vocation, for the kind of person I want to become. (We will need to aim high for the kind of character we truly want to become. This is vital to our ultimate success.)

4. Have only one person in the household write checks, or make debits, on each checking account. Keep an accurate running balance of the accounts at **all times**. Both spouses should know what is happening in all family financial accounts. A check should **never** be written that will overdraw an account, even if we are positive that we will be able to cover the overdraft before the check gets back to the bank. (We really can't run that fast!)

5. Pray before **all purchases**—even food. We must remember that there is a difference between what we need and what we want.

6. No credit card purchases unless we can pay them at the end of the month as part of our financial plan. No use of charge accounts. No items on lay away, unless it's part of the family's budget. (This last phrase is helpful to think through.)

7. No purchase over $______________ (an agreed upon amount) without consulting spouse and prayer.

8. No purchase over $ __________________ without consulting spouse, prayer, and waiting ______ days before making the purchase. Often those "big deals" are not so necessary after two or three weeks.

9. Make a list before going shopping. Stick to the list. (Some items on sale may be permissible if they fit into the family's budget and family menus.)

10. Save for major purchases. Use financing very sparingly. (Note # 6 above.)

11. Treat saving as a fixed expense. It should be a regular part of the family's budget.

12. If both spouses are earning income, establish a budget that requires only one of the incomes to make ends meet. (This will probably be a long-term goal.)

13. If you have children, help them to set up a budget too. This will teach them financial responsibility (and that Mom and Dad do not have endless supplies of cash!).

14. If children are still in the home, share with them as they grow older how the income is spent and in this way help them learn to become wise stewards.

15. Understand that some day the Lord will call for an accounting of all our investments, our expenditures, and what we have done with our talents, our time, and our influence.

16. When we learn to live simply, we discover that less really is more.

(This list was adapted from a discussion in a conference with James C. Green about Christian stewardship. Used by permission.)

Home Assignments

- Memorize the Key Verse (Ps 96:8).
- Ask your accountability partner to share some of his/her experiences in the stewardship of money.

Step 11

Stewardship of Time and Talents

Key Verse

"Live wisely among those who are not believers, and make the most of every opportunity." —Colossians 4:5 NLT

Introduction

This is a parable of time: When we were born, a bank account was opened in our name. No one knows how much is in the account. We can spend as much of the account as often as we want for whatever we want, but some day that bank account will be depleted. Now, how are we going to spend it??

Time is a possession we often forget to give to the Lord, yet we need to be wise managers of our time as much as anything else we have. Although every Christ-follower wants to be involved in God's work, idleness, secondary concerns, or too much entertainment can rob God of our precious gift of time.

Abundant living requires finding a balance between work and play, worship and rest, relaxation and purposeful activity. Some of us push ourselves so much that we are fatigued and irritable. Does that please the Lord? Some of us feel guilty because we fail to keep our commitments to God's work, time and again. Is that any better? The abundant life is characterized by a well-balanced use of our time.

Our goal is to work without being driven and play without feeling guilty. When your day/week/life is finished, you will not have done everything you wanted or planned to do, but you can say, "Lord, I have invested my time in a way that I believe is pleasing in Your sight." That knowledge will bring a genuine sense of joy and fulfillment and great peace.

As a part of daily prayer, share with the Lord your needs, struggles, and concerns about your time usage. Seek to set realistic goals for the activities of each day. Prioritize your time on the basis of what you believe is most important in God's plan for you to do. Discipline yourself to stay with that task until it is completed before moving on to other important tasks.

There will always be interruptions, of course. When they come, you will need to decide prayerfully what is most important at the time. Jesus often used interruptions for significant ministries. See if you can do the same. Especially try to see the needs of your spouse, children, and parents not as interruptions but as God-given ministries to persons in your care. They won't always need you according to your schedule, so be sensitive to the calling of God during each day. The Holy Spirit will guide you. Make this a guilt-free journey; you will need grace here too.

Let's also think about our stewardship of the talents and natural abilities God has given us. Seek to discover your best gifts and use them for the glory of God. Here are some advantages of knowing what your talents are:

- You know what you do best, so you feel good about giving yourself in those ways.
- You are not obliged to say yes to every opportunity that comes along.
- When you need to step up and do something that you are not gifted to do, you can make it a short-term commitment.
- You can always put your best into what God calls you to do. You can avoid bringing shoddy workmanship or a negative spirit to any task.
- You discover many ways to use your gifts in God's service: men's fellowships, missionary circles, prayer groups, mentoring children/youth, caring for orphans, helping widows and single moms, Scouting, coaching, singing in the church choir (or worship team), teaching, community service projects, taking elderly people to the doctor, and many more.
- If you employ your best gifts for God's service, you can take time to be alone with God without feeling guilty because you are not "doing more."

Bible Study

I. Godly time management

A. Read Psalm 90 and list the principles of time management that you find there, focusing on verses 1–2, 10, 12, 14, and 17.

____

____

____

B. Read Ephesians 5:15–17. What does it say about the need for focus in your use of time?

____

____

C. Philippians 4:19 says God will supply everything you need to serve Him. How do you think this applies to your time and talents?

____

____

D. Reflect on Psalm 138:8 and Proverbs 16:9. How might these verses comfort you on days when all of your plans seem to go wrong?

____

____

> **We always make time for things that are important enough.**
> **—Ted Engstrom**

II. Tithing your time and talents

A. There are 168 hours in a week. A tithe (one tenth) of that time is 16.8 hours. Here's a suggested way of allocating your week's time to give a tithe of it to God:

1. If you work 50 hours per week and tithe on that income, subtract one-tenth of that time (in this example, 5 hours) from your time tithe.
2. Count the time you invest in worship and church activities as a part of your tithe of time. (Include travel time.)
3. Count the time you spend in Bible reading, meditation, and prayer each day. If it is 30 minutes a day, for example, subtract 3.5 hours from your weekly tithe of time.

B. Use the remaining time for personal ministries to your neighbors and others who need you.

We encourage you to use the worksheet at the end of this week's session to compute your time/talent tithe for the week.

Home Assignments

- Memorize the Key Verse (Col 4:5).
- With your accountability partner, complete the "Worksheet for a Weekly Tithe of Time and Talents"

Worksheet for a Weekly Tithe of Time and Talents

Activity	Time Tithed	Tithe Remaining (Subtract from 16.8 Hrs)
I work _______ / wk. (10% of time worked if you tithe your work income)	________________	________________
I invest _______/wk. (Church activities)	________________	________________
I invest _______/wk. (Devotional time w/God)	________________	________________
I spend _______/wk.	________________	________________

giving of myself in neighborhood ministries in the name of Christ (listening to a child read, Bible studies, prayer groups, "coffee friendships," and so on).

Any other ministry to which God may be calling me that will enable me to invest more of myself, my time, and my gifts for the sake of eternity:

____

____

My Weekly Tithe of Time (Should Be 16.8 Hours or More): ___________

Step 12

Stewardship of Our Relationships

Key Verse

"A new command I give you: Love one another. As I have loved you, so you must love one another. By this all men will know that you are my disciples if you love one another." —John 13:34–35 NIV1984

Introduction

When we come to Christ, we begin to grow in divine grace and knowledge. As we grow in grace, we will become more kind and courteous in our relationships with one another. We cannot expect unbelievers to see the world from a grace perspective, but it is vital that Christ-followers seek to make God's grace work in their circles.

Have you ever seen a congregation where people did not treat one another with divine grace? Such a church is characterized by discontent, back-biting, ill-will, wrangling, and all kinds of troubled relationships. This is not the kind of community that Christ expects the church to be.

James 3:13–18 compares the qualities godly wisdom and worldly wisdom. Notice the difference between these lists in Table 1. (These lists are based on the NIV's rendering of verses 15-17.)

Regardless of where you are on your spiritual journey, you have the challenge of treating others with sacrificial love, kindness, and good manners. In other words, you can manage all of the relationships God has given you with a Christlike spirit. What does the New Testament have to say about how to make grace work?

Table 1: Godly wisdom versus worldly wisdom.

Worldly Wisdom	Godly Wisdom
Earthly	Pure
Unspiritual	Peace-loving
Devilish	Considerate
Envious	Submissive
Selfish	Merciful
Ambitious	Fruitful
Disorderly	Impartial
Evil-doing	Sincere

Bible Study

New Testament guidelines for grace-filled relationships

A. "Speaking the truth in love"

1. How did the prophet Nathan do this with King David (2 Sam 12:1–13)?

   ____

   ____

2. How did the apostle Paul do this with the apostle Peter (Gal 2:11–16)?

   ____

   ____

3. Describe a current relationship where you need to "speak the truth in love."

   ____

   ____

B. "Hearing the truth in love"

1. How did Saul of Tarsus hear the truth in love when Christ confronted him (Acts 22:1–11)?

   ____

   ____

2. How did the Jewish believers in Jerusalem hear the truth in love when the apostles opposed their demands (Acts 15:5–14, 30–32)?

____

____

3. Describe a current relationship where you need to hear the truth in love.

____

____

C. "Serving one another in love"

1. In the lesson on ordinances, we saw how Jesus washed His disciples' feet at the Last Supper. Why did He do this (John 13:12–17)?

____

____

2. The apostle Paul told his Christian friends in Galatia to stop "biting and devouring one other." What did he say they should do instead (Gal 5:13–15)?

____

____

3. Describe a current relationship where you need to serve someone else in love.

____

____

D. "Forgiving one another in love"

1. Why does Jesus say we should forgive those who harm us (Matt 6:13–15)?

____

____

2. Why should we forgive other Christians who harm us (Col 3:12–14)?

____

____

3. Describe a current relationship where you need to forgive someone.

____

____

E. "Submitting to one another"

1. In your own congregation, who would be equivalent to the people that Paul encouraged the Corinthian believers to submit to (1 Cor 16:15–16)?

____

____

2. Who do you think are the "leaders" that the writer of Hebrews says we should submit to (Heb 13:15–17)?

____

____

3. Identify a spiritual leader to whom you should submit at this stage of your faith journey.

____

____

F. "Encouraging one another in love"

1. Restate Hebrews 10:24–25 in your own words:

____

____

2. The book of Acts often refers to a Jewish Christian from Cyprus named Joseph who had the nickname of Barnabas (Son of Encouragement). Read these references to Joseph's ministry and explain why you think the church called him this.

Acts 4:32–37

____

____

Acts 9:26–30

____

____

Acts 11:19–26

____

____

Acts 15:36–41

____

____

3. Make a list of some people who could use your encouragement (young, old, and in between)

G. "Bearing one another's burdens"

1. Read Galatians 6:2–5. What do you think is the difference between carrying someone's else's "burden" (v 2 NIV1984) and carrying your own "load" (v 5 NIV1984)?

____

____

2. What are some burdens of life that God never intended for people to carry alone?

____

____

3. Identify one or two people whose burdens you could lift this week:

____

____

Bearing One Another's Burdens

(An illustration from the author's life)

Many years ago, my wife was terminally ill with cancer. We were in the prime of life and still had one son in his early teens at home. With the duties of a busy ministry, caring for my wife, and trying to be a good father to my teenage son, the situation became more than I could bear.

The ladies in our church appointed someone to visit my wife and learn what her dietary needs were. They then began preparing dinner for us three evenings each week. The meals were thoughtfully prepared, timely delivered, and lovingly given—in generous portions. Other ladies dressed my wife's hair and did innumerable small kindnesses for her until she went to be with the Lord.

As long as I live, my heart will overflow with gratitude because these godly women stepped up to do such loving things for our family when we were in great pain. I get a lump in my throat even now as I tell you how the people of that congregation were willing to bear one another's burdens.

Home Assignments

- Memorize the Key Verse (John 13:34–35).
- Tell your accountability partner about a time when someone has borne your burden (physical, spiritual, or emotional). What did that experience tell you about that person's relationship with Jesus Christ?
- Identify someone whose burden you can lift this week.

Step 13

Stewardship of the Gospel

Key Verse

"You did not choose me, but I chose you and appointed you to go and bear fruit—fruit that will last." —John 15:16a NIV1984

Introduction

You and I have been entrusted with the good news of Jesus Christ. What will we do with it? Shall we enjoy the benefits of eternal, abundant life for ourselves? Or will we tell others so they can share the blessings with us? Whether we will share the gospel, and how we share it, is the most important stewardship of a Christ-follower's life.

Your total being is a witness to the life-changing power of God. He created you, and now you have invited Christ to reign in your life so that you become God's spiritual child. This is huge. Your actions, your thoughts, and your desires have been changed (and continue to change) from being self-centered to being Christ-centered.

Simply being yourself—your redeemed self—is vital to sharing Jesus Christ with others. God does not expect you to imitate any other person's methods or style of personal evangelism. God has worked uniquely in your life. Allow Him to use your uniqueness to touch other people's lives for His glory.

Allow me to share what this means in my own life: I want my life to be continually examined by God so that the way I think, work, and talk reflect His grace in my life. When I go to work, I will be a faithful worker because I am working for Him. At home, I am a caring husband and father because it is what He wants me to be. I discipline myself to form the right attitudes, habits, and thoughts because as a Christ-follower, these things demonstrate to the world the kind of Lord I serve. The more time I spend with Christ, the more I take on His own characteristics. The more I depend on Christ and the power of the Holy Spirit in my life, the less difficult this discipline becomes and the more these characteristics become a natural part of me.

This is not to say that temptation ceases to appeal to me, but with God's Spirit in me, I now have the power to resist it. And by resisting temptation, I demonstrate the power of God in my life.

I cannot expect to tell others about Jesus Christ very convincingly if my attitudes and actions deny Him. I know my life is being watched by other people. My actions and attitudes tell them more about my Lord than anything I might say. I have known a few people who could speak a beautifully worded testimony at church while their spouses told quite a different story. So I must not live a double life. I must not act without integrity.

When I have blown it, I need to say, "I spoke out of turn (or with the wrong attitude) earlier. I am sorry. I was clearly out of line. The Holy Spirit has prompted me to come and make this right." Most people respect that kind of honesty. They already know when I've stepped out of line. So my witness to the power of Jesus Christ will have integrity only if I share honestly with them and offer my sincere apology.

So how do we tell others about Jesus Christ? We can simply say in our own unique way how Christ has changed us, our attitudes, our desires, and our behavior. To be credible, we need to talk very naturally (without using pious words or preachy tone) about what Christ is doing for us now. We can relax as we share the story, because we know that Christ's Spirit is still transforming us into the very image of Christ, and that same Spirit will convey the truth to the hearts of those who hear us.

If you saw someone drowning in a river and you could rescue the person, you would try. People around you who do not know Jesus Christ are in a much more serious situation. Their eternal destiny is at stake. So pray for them and share the story of what Christ is doing in your own life; then leave the results with God. Raise the issue again lovingly if the Holy Spirit prompts you, but you don't want to be strident or combative in your approach. Just be yourself and tell your own gospel story.

Bible Study

I. New Testament symbols of sharing the good news

A. In Matthew 5:13, Jesus says we are "the salt of the earth." Read that passage in context and then explain what you think He means:

B. In Matthew 5:14–16, Jesus says we are "the light of the world" and "a lamp" in the darkness. Again, read this passage in context and explain what you think He means by this.

II. Qualifications to share the good news

A. Luke 8:38–39 says that Jesus healed a man who "begged to go with him," but Jesus sent him home. Why?

B. How were the twelve disciples qualified to tell others about Jesus (John 15:26–27)?

III. The essence of the good news

A. According to 2 Corinthians 5:16–21, what is the essence of our message when we tell others about Jesus?

B. Read the apostle Paul's account of what Jesus Christ was doing in his life (Phil 3:12–14). Make a list of phrases that jump out at you as the essence of what He was saying.

IV. How the Master did it

Reflect on the account of Jesus' conversation with the Samaritan woman at Jacob's well (John 4:1–42). Why do you suppose Jesus got through to her? What were the ingredients of His powerful witness?

____

____

____

____

V. Benefits of sharing the good news

A. Read each of the following passages and then explain in your own words how we will benefit if we share our Christian testimony with others:

1. Romans 10:9–10

   ____

   ____

2. 1 Peter 3:14–17

   ____

   ____

3. Revelation 12:10–11

   ____

   ____

Home Assignments

- Memorize the Key Verse (John 15:16)
- Write out your own account of what Christ has done in your life. Make it five paragraphs in length. Ask your accountability partner to help you with writing this out.

  a. 1 paragraph about your life before you came to Christ

  ____

  ____

b. 1 paragraph about what happened when you surrendered your life to Christ

c. 3 paragraphs about how your life continues to change since you came to Christ. The heaviest emphasis should be on the present and the future.

Suggested Reading

Aldrich, Sandra P. *Bless Your Socks Off: Unleashing the Power of Encouragement.* Wheaton, IL: Tyndale House Publishers, 1998.

Callen, Barry L. *The Prayer of Holiness-Hungry People: A Disciple's Guide to the Lord's Prayer.* Anderson, IN: Francis Asbury Press, 2011.

Oldham, W. Dale. *How to Grow Spiritually.* Anderson, IN: Warner Press, 2007.

———. *Living Close to God.* Anderson, IN: Warner Press, 2007.

Oswalt, John N. *Called to Be Holy: A Biblical Perspective.* Anderson, IN: Francis Asbury Press, 1999

Shumate, Charles R., and Sherrill D. Hayes, eds. *Discover Your Gifts.* Anderson, IN: Warner Press, 1982, 1990.

Stafford, Gilbert W. *Theology for Disciples.* Anderson, IN: Warner Press, 1996.

Thompson, David L. *Bible Study That Works.* Anderson, IN: Francis Asbury Press, 1982, 1994.

Printed in the USA
CPSIA information can be obtained
at www.ICGtesting.com
JSHW050344140124
55279JS00010B/65

9 781593 175771